AURORA ABERDEEN

THE LAWS OF ABUNDANCE

THE INTERGALACTIC BESTSELLER

www.middlefinger.press

Book Design by Will Clarke // Cover image ©iStockPhoto

1st Edition
10 9 8 7 6 5 4 3 2 1

(paperback) ISBN: 978-0-9726588-6-7

(e-book) ISBN: 978-0-9726588-7-4

TO ALL THE DOERS & DREAMERS & NO-IN-BETWEENERS!

This book was written for those of you who believe in magic.

If you don't believe in magic,
this book might seem
outrageous.

"Impossible!"

Maybe even farcical.

And for this I am truly sorry.

What a cruel irony that you hold
the greatest gift that The Universe
has ever bestowed upon you
and yet you might never truly open it.

How sad for you.

But alas, there are no mistakes.

Only lessons!

YOUR BRAIN IS A TIME MACHINE.

IT RECALLS THE PAST AS EASILY

AS IT ENVISIONS THE FUTURE.

YOUR BRAIN IS ALSO A MONEY MACHINE.

ONLY PROBLEM IS

MOST FOLKS HAVE FORGOTTEN THEIR PIN CODE.

THE LAWS OF ABUNDANCE WILL ALLOW YOU

TO ACCESS UNIVERSAL FLOW.

CASH WILL EXPLODE

LIKE CHERRY BLOSSOMS IN APRIL.

NOT HYPERBOLE.

OR METAPHOR.

THIS ACTUALLY HAPPENS TO ME

WHEN I WORK THE LAWS

THAT SAVED ME FROM CANCER.

YOU TOO

CAN BECOME

A MASTER

MANIFESTER.

YOUR

DREAMS

WILL

FALL

AT

YOUR FEET

LIKE

FRUIT

DROPPING

FROM

THE

TREES.

WHAT WILL YOU DO WITH IT ALL?

THE LAWS OF ABUNDANCE

HAVE BEEN CHANNELED

NOT FROM ALIENS

OR SO-CALLED MASTERS

BUT FROM INFINITE INTELLIGENCE.

THE UNI-VERSE.

THE ONE SONG.

ALSO CONGRATULATIONS.

IF YOU ARE READING THIS BOOK

YOU HAVE ATTRACTED

THE LAWS OF ABUNDANCE

INTO YOUR LIFE.

AGAIN MORE PROOF

YOU ARE

MANIFESTING REALITY

ALL THE TIME.

THERE ARE NO SECRETS TO MANIFESTATION.

ONLY THE LAWS OF ABUNDANCE.

YOU HAVE ALWAYS KNOWN THE LAWS.

JUST MAYBE FORGOT

THEM.

THE LAWS OF ABUNDANCE ARE THE RAILROAD TRACKS FOR THE REALITY TRAIN.

VISUALIZE YOURSELF:

"THE LITTLE ENGINE THAT COULD."

SEE YOUR DREAMS AS THE TRAIN TRACKS

YOU ARE LAYING DOWN ON THE EARTH'S CROOKED BACK

FOR THE SILVER LOCOMOTIVE OF DESTINY

TO BLOW ITS STEAM WHISTLE

AND CARRY YOU AWAY.

FIRST LAW OF ABUNDANCE:

YOU EXIST IN THE MIDST OF A MIRACLE.

You shouldn't exist. By the numbers that is. The odds that you live on this small blue planet reading this exact sentence in a book entitled *THE LAWS OF ABUNDANCE* are literally astronomical. The probability that you are a sentient being born on a planet with the gravity and atmosphere to support life after the violent heat and velocity of The Big Bang is unfathomable.

Do you realize how infinitesimally small the probability was that our Universe spewed forth from the yawning abyss of nothingness?

That we "Big Banged" into existence from a Multiverse of Infinite Possibilities?

The improbability of the initial density conditions needed for our Universe to cool and form planets and stars is beyond anything you could imagine. The Goldilocks conditions of gravity that coagulated into galaxies and life-giving planets are so mathematically impossible that most astrophysicists who have researched them have a hard time believing their own calculations.

Put aside the faith-shattering probabilities of the Big Bang, take a clean sheet of paper and calculate the probability of the meiosis crossovers and billions upon billions of DNA mutations that took us from primordial sludge to placental mammals to these bizarre, big-brained, naked apes: homo sapiens who drive Teslas and take selfies.

It's all just as mathematically impossible.

In fact, the list of reasons why you shouldn't be alive at all—from nuclear bombs to antibiotic resistant staph infections — is mind-blowing and terrifying.

But alas, here we are.

The impossible made possible.

Beings lucky enough to live on the friendliest edges of a seemingly infinite explosion known as The Universe.

And this is nothing short of a miracle.

DO YOU SEE THE UNIVERSE AS HALF-FULL?

OR HALF-EMPTY?

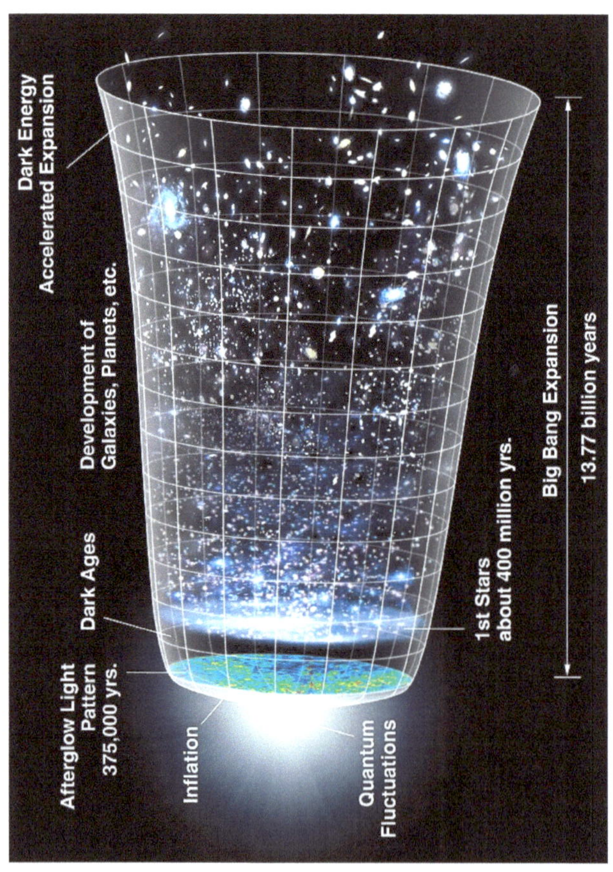

THE BIG BANG courtesy of NASA

But who among you awakens each morning and says, "Thank you, Universe! For allowing me to exist when most things will never even become a flicker in someone's eye. Our reality is virtually haunted by the ghosts of never-born galaxies, stars, planets, species, people, and ideas.

What waits in the shadows of nothingness, of never having happened, is legion.

THAT'S THE TRAGIC MATH AND SACRED GEOMETRY OF PURE POTENTIALITY.

Metatron's Cube Image by Szlávics Alexa/ Courtesy of Wikimedia Commons

Simply being allowed to manifest in 3D reality is one of the rarest gifts in all the probabilities that can be calculated. Even your death is a gift. Because most things will never be born, and therefore, never die.

And yet you act like life is no big deal. Your entitlement and lack of gratitude are quite frankly stunning. You actually have no awe. No real working concept that you have against all odds manifested a brain to be reading this very sentence. That you have grown a heart, quietly beating, pumping your blood, keeping you alive. You act like you have always existed and that you always will. But I have news for you: You haven't and you won't.

As rare of a gift that your existence is, it is, after all, finite. Growing even more precious day by day, because in one split second, you will *cease to exist in this dimension*. You will be like all the other things that never existed. Your life will be over and your body will return to the void.

And yet.

Do you really treat your own manifestation in this Universe as the miracle that it is? No, you act like everything is annoying and stupid. You ignore sunsets. You take for granted the oxygen molecules that have been generously provided to support your carbon-based life-form. You are cruel to so many other living beings all around you. You are petulant and impatient. And worst of all, you are bored.

You lack wonder and avoid awe. Instead, you complain about taxes and traffic and coworkers who get on your nerves. Your pants are too tight. The milk has soured. Your coffee is cold! Your toilets have overflowed. Your phone is dead. Oh, no! Life is terrible. Wah-wah.

Get over yourself. How do you think all those unborn people feel? (They don't feel anything because they don't exist!) Homo Sapiens have spent eons making up fake miracles and singing hymns to them and repeating their myths in their liturgies when in all actuality they are blind to the most wondrous miracle of all.

WE ARE ALIVE WHEN MOST THINGS WILL NEVER BE ALIVE!

Hypergiant Star Canis Majoris courtesy of NASA

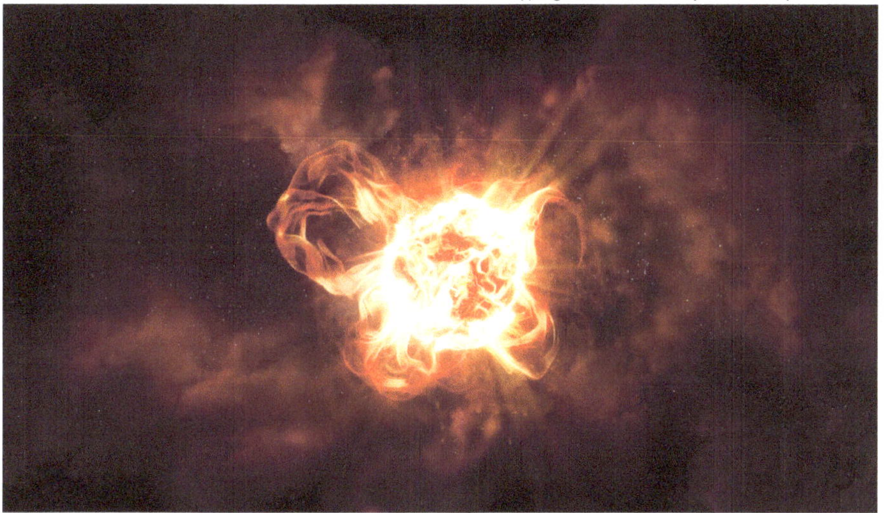

If we are to work together, first you must admit that **you exist in midst of a miracle.** This is THE FIRST LAW OF ABUNDANCE, and until you have constant awareness of this immutable law, there is really nothing for us to do together.

If you are unable to grasp this prime concept, you might as well close this book now and go fiddle with your iPhone or complain about the weather or whatever you do to waste time.

For without total understanding of the First Law, there is no need to go on.

Why waste these sacred words on the closed mind of a Philistine?

Why join you in your ennui and despair?

THE MILKY WAY courtesy of NASA

SECOND LAW OF ABUNDANCE:

WHAT YOU COMPLAIN ABOUT YOU BRING ABOUT.

Let's talk about your complaining. It's a real problem for me and for most of the beings in The Universe.

You want to know why?

Because "What you complain about you bring about." Likewise, what is as equally outrageous and annoying is how people are scared to say their dreams and desires out loud (knocking on wood and whatnot), hoping they "don't jinx it." This is utterly ridiculous and quite honestly obnoxious.

PROCLAIM YOUR DREAMS!

The more outrageous, the better. The more you speak of your success, the more you confess with your mouth, the more positive vibrations you will put out into the Cosmos, and the more it will all come back to you. Fearing to speak of your wishes, dreams, and desires will actually block them from manifesting. It drives me crazy that most folks still do not get this.

Even toddlers get this. However, grown men and women do not. A child at play might say aloud, "I want a red balloon!" Then out of nowhere, a red balloon floats down from the sky, settles just in the grasp of the child's hands. Oh, the giggling and the joy and the gratitude of such a child! The Universe is so drawn to this child-like wonder and will provide even more miracles because it feels so appreciated and loved. The vibes are just so delicious. Who doesn't like to play and be appreciated?

WHO DOESN'T LOVE GIGGLING?

But alas, when you are that pure and that young, The Universe will always meet you where you are and put all manifest your every whim. Once negativity creeps into your monkey mind, once you grow up and put on a suit and get a "real job" that's when all the complaining starts. That's when you become a "fun sponge." You suck all the jelly out of the donut. And The Universe can see that you are no longer that wonderstruck child.

The tell-tale sign that you have become a "fun sponge" is your regular attendance at so-called "happy hours," where you and your colleagues order half-priced margaritas and dollar IPAs while you lament the drama of your sad, office lives. The complaints spew forth like rockets of verbal diarrhea! Of course, the once kind and playful Universe is repelled by these pathetic, afterwork get-togethers.

DISGUSTED REALLY.

Who wouldn't be? Worse still, The Universe is now hurt and sad (Yes, The Universe has feelings. The Universe is after all ultimate consciousness. It *invented* feelings.) So now when you reach out with an urgent wish or need, the once friendly and playful Universe retreats from your desperate embrace. However, like a faithful, beaten dog, The Universe still delivers. It drops newspapers at your feet, full of all the tragedy and disaster that your negative thoughts have conjured. The Universe dutifully brings you all the car crashes and cancer diagnoses and divorces that your untamed mind obsesses over. And I should know; I manifested the cancer and the car wrecks and more before I discovered *THE LAWS OF ABUNDANCE*.

That's because we manifest everything that we do not want with our complaints. Now that I practice *THE LAWS*, I am simply flummoxed as to how people do not see this. But alas, most people don't. Which is why I have had to sit down and write this book while my dear friends, Nancy and Donny Regan, have taken my boat out and are now waterskiing without me while I am back at my lake house, still in my bathing suit, dripping wet as I type out *THE LAWS* that have saved my life. (Keep reading! Maybe take notes! They will save your life too!)

"I don't know much about being a millionaire, but I'll bet I'd be darling at it."

DOROTHY PARKER
as channeled at
The Cassadaga Book Fair
March 24, 2008

YOUR WORDS ARE VIBRATIONS THAT YOU PUT OUT INTO THE UNIVERSE.

Your tongue and lips literally manipulate the air molecules all around you with your words. And newsflash: Time-Space is like this great big metaphysical megaphone. It amplifies your vibrations (your words, your moods, your thoughts) and plays them back to you in the form of an ever-unfolding 3D reality. A "Toroidal Loop of Reality" that is eternal.

The everyday negative words you speak—*the gossiping, the griping, the groaning*— manifest all the things you complain about. We've all met the person who is sick all the time or who is constantly losing their keys or their jobs or their lovers, and they are always bitching and complaining about how "life sucks." This is why. They are manifesting their own negative experiences. It's as glaringly obvious as the sun in the sky.

Instead of complaining and cursing what is and shall always be, try *blessing it*. Try shifting your perspective. Try manifesting a different reality by saying things like:

"God Bless, I'm running late for my plane. What a fun adventure missing my flight will be! Oh, the new souls I will meet because if this and the problems I will learn to solve. This is all just part of the winding journey of my soul. Not the melodramatic frustration that society wants me to think it is. Even if the airline charges me $500 change fees to make another flight. Just an illusion because I can create $1000 in some other part of my life by merely building a vision board. So I am good. I am more than good."

Or:

"Oh, I tested positive for the flu? How curious? What part of me am I not giving enough love to? Hmm. Let me lean into my feelings and see why I am running this fever. This is so interesting how my body and mind are connected. Oh, look, there it is! I have discovered why I had agreed to let myself get sick. I didn't want to go to the job that I hate, and I am self-sabotaging. I really should be a painter of seascapes, not some boring accountant like good old Dad wanted me to be! What a breakthrough! Just facing my strangled emotions, I feel better. My fever has broken. My flu seems to be going away and I am realizing that I am powerful enough to heal myself with the infinite love that I keep forgetting is all around me. I am practically bathing in good fortune and white light! I will quit my job as a CPA, buy some oil paints, and move to Maine, and I will do so knowing The Universe will provide for me!"

See how with a little imagination, you can regain control of your own life? This is a master-level meditation that literally changes the very fabric of Time-Space all around you. Try it. Go ahead. I'll wait right here while you do.

WHAT YOU RESIST IN THE UNIVERSE, PERSISTS. THIS IS TRIPLY SO DURING A MERCURY IN RETROGRADE.

THE PLANET MERCURY courtesy of NASA

These particular astrological moments are not times to press forward. A retrograde is a time to repair your nets, not cast them upon the sea. In fact, I hate hearing people bitch and moan and blame Mercury for their crappy decisions. All this drama around a minor celestial event is so unnecessary. Once again, any mishap that occurs during this period is on you. And it just shows how much people do not understand The Universe and how it works.

LET ME CHANNEL MY FAVORITE SPIRIT GUIDE, F. SCOTT FITZGERALD, AND SEE WHAT HE HAS TO SAY ABOUT THIS:

"When Mercury falls backwards in the sky, that is the Cosmos telling you that you are in a season of reflection and relaxation, not striving and building.

1921— Francis Scott Fitzgerald who is dead, but speaks to me across the Spirit Plane. Image courtesy of Wikimedia Commons.

Retrogrades are times to stop and rethink your life. Traveling or moving forward during a retrograde is ludicrous. It is pissing in the wind! It's like planting sunflower seeds in a blizzard and wondering why nothing spouts in the snow because it's not the season for that kind of activity, you idiot! (F. Scott's words, not mine!) There is a season for everything."

What F. Scott has taught me is that "Mercury in Retrograde" is merely a season. It's not personal. So stop complaining about it. You are making this already frustrating moment worse for everyone who has to listen to you gripe about a rather minor celestial event.

Mercury in Retrograde is a good time to do anything with a "re" prefix. Re-lax, re-wind, re-vise, re-think, re-alize, re-imagine, re-write, re-work, re-evaluate, re-cline, re-visit, re-turn, etc. All things, according to F. Scott, that can best be perfected in the South of France. Preferably Cannes.

RETROGRADES ARE NOT A GOOD TIME TO MAKE DECISIONS OR AGREEMENTS OR TRAVEL. STAY PUT!

And stop complaining. "Oh, Mercury is in Retrograde. Oh, no!" If you understood how the solar system worked, you wouldn't have anything to complain about because you would be taking this time to relax and rewind, not travel and press forward.

You would realize you are doing all of this to yourself. Because you are ultimately weaving your life experiences with your own cry-baby thoughts and annoying complaints.

BEWARE: THE NEGATIVE REINFORCEMENT OF SELF-HELP BOOKS & SPIRITUAL DEVICES.

F. Scott told me that this May 1, 1920 Rockwell cover of *The Saturday Evening Post* shows how cute underestimation of spiritual devises can lead to real dangers. *The Exorcist (1971)* may have never been written had it not been for this cover popularizing the Ouija.

Many among you have what you call a "cuss jar." A glass container upon which you deposit coins every time you say a filthy word. This self-help trend is as dangerous as children playing with Ouija Boards.

Sadly cuss jars are maybe even more dangerous. They increase negativity because they reward you for your negative speech and thinking. (It's own form of demonic possession for sure!)

You are literally paying yourself for cussing.

THIS IS CALLED NEGATIVE REINFORCEMENT.

Cuss jars as well as all your self-help books that recommend their use are just another form of self-punishment masquerading as self-discipline. This kind of thinking stops nothing. It actually reinforces your bad behavior. You will actually cuss more by using these insidious jars and books. Eventually you will take your jars overflowing with nickels, quarters, and dimes to some poor bank teller. From this same bank account, you will use these cuss jar funds to buy yourself dinner at The Cheesecake Factory or a new throw rug from West Elm — or worse, Ikea!

Cuss jars and self-help books do not work the way you think they do. They are both satanic devices. As are all forms of self-help that you try to employ because they are just a form of negative thinking dressed up as enlightenment!

The amount of negative thoughts being woven into our current time stream because of people's love of Ouija Boards, self-help books, and cuss jars is breathtaking. To be honest, keeping a cuss jar and reading self-help are forms of metaphysical sadomasochism. And you must stop it immediately. So gather up all the cuss jars in your house. Go right now and throw all your self-help books into your bathtub. Fill the tub with cold water until the books are nothing but pulp. Then hold your cuss jar over your head and proclaim:

"Negative words! You no longer hold sway over my tongue or my life!" And then crash the jar on the floor and do not clean it up. Live with the broken glass and the coins on your floor. And let yourself experience the real consequence of your negative thoughts. After a week or so of stepping around the broken glass and coins, sweep it all up and bury it near sweet water. Burn a yellow candle and sing, "You are my Sunshine" three times. Seriously, do this now. I am determined to stop the plague that are cuss jars in this country.

If you do not employ a "cuss jar" or own a library full of self-help books or a Ouija board, consider yourself exempt from this exercise. Luckily, you are a more evolved soul than most Americans, and you don't need to be retrained from such odious, self-destructive behaviors. But do not smack your lips in self-satisfaction; I am sure you have plenty of other bad habits I will need to help you break.

I feel certain, cuss jar or not, there is more work ahead for us! After all, you can never be too rich or too skinny! More *LAWS OF ABUNDANCE* still await your mastery.

So keep reading.

EXCELSIOR!

THIRD LAW OF ABUNDANCE: **THE RICH DON'T BITCH.**

Now, this might seem like a repeat of "The Second Law," but it is not. Your annoying habit of constant complaining is a completely separate issue from the reality that "The Rich Don't Bitch." The very fact that you might not see this right off the bat speaks volumes about where you are on your journey to abundance and enlightenment.

But alas, if you intuitively already understood the nuances of *THE LAWS OF ABUNDANCE*, I wouldn't have to sit here in my bathrobe, sipping my Sanka while I channel The Universe. If you already lived by *THE LAWS OF ABUNDANCE* and truly understood your own role in creating your reality, my book wouldn't have found its way into your hands. Then I could instead be out enjoying beachside mimosas with my dear friends Nancy and Donny Regan, but alas, my job has been assigned by the Fates: So here I am. Typing away like the recording Angel. Elucidating more of *THE LAWS for my dear readers*. Ready to help The Universe retrain the entire human race on how the "Toroidal Loops of Reality" truly work before it is too late.

So back to becoming one of "The Rich." And why you are not one of us. Yet.

I THINK F. SCOTT FITZGERALD PUT IT BEST WHEN I FIRST CHANNELED HIM AT HEIDI KLUM'S 2009 HALLOWEEN PARTY:

"Let me tell you about the very rich. They are different from you and me.

They possess and enjoy early, and it does something to them, makes them soft where we are hard, and cynical where we are trustful, in a way that, unless you were born rich, it is very difficult to understand.

They think, deep in their hearts, that they are better than we are because we had to discover the compensations and refuges of life for ourselves.

Even when they enter deep into our world or sink below us, they still think that they are better than we are.

They are different."

Photo Courtesy WikiMedia Commons

June 4, 1937 — Francis Scott Fitzgerald photographed by Carl van Vechten.

WE ARE INDEED DIFFERENT FROM YOU. BECAUSE:

1) **We possess and enjoy early.** What's not to enjoy about manifesting your dreams into reality? So what if we are precocious babies? (Remember: The Universe loves the wonder-stuck demands of a child.)

2) **We are soft.** But do not mistake our softness for weakness. The rich are not weak. But we do welcome softness into our lives. We cultivate the suppleness of luxury. We know how to bask in it and because we are so appreciative of soft lives, The Universe brings us more luxury to rest our heads upon.

3) **We are cynical**. Now do not even try to pretend this is a bad thing. Healthy cynicism is merely mental armor that keeps one from being easily duped by flimflam men. If you want to be rich, hone your cynicism, sharpen it, polish it, and then don this golden chest plate and helmet in all your negotiations and dealings that involve money.

4) **We think we are better than you**. Well, of course we do. After all, what we think about, we bring about. Just think it and make it so!

Now some might say this was F. Scott's critique of the wealthy, but it most certainly was not. Fitzgerald was obsessed with us. He courted the noblesse oblige of countless millionaire patrons like his dear friends, Sara and Gerald Murphy. Oh, the romps they had with Zelda on the French Riviera! The tender nights on the moon swept beaches. The popping of Champagne! The sloshing of gin. The shimmy-shimmy shakes. The Foxtrots and Charlestons.

But I digress.

The point I was making was that Fitzgerald studied the rich. He was obsessed, wanted to be one of us himself.

1917, F. Scott ("the minister"), probably tipsy on bathtub gin in this photo, loved throwing parties, putting on silly costumes, and performing bawdy skits with his "very rich" friends. Courtesy of the Minnesota Historical Society/ Wikimedia Commons

And it is with this insight that one should read all of Fitzgerald's works. Particularly his long-lost short story entitled, **The I.O.U."** This story in particular is the key to everything I have ever channeled from F. Scott Fitzgerald. For his keen novelist's eye provides us all with something of an Illuminated roadmap to learning the true mindset of the "very rich." And it will set you on your journey of activating *THE LAWS OF ABUNDANCE* for yourself and your heirs.

Once I started channeling F. Scott Fitzgerald on a regular basis, once I truly took the time to understand what he stood for, I had a major mental breakthrough. Total lighting bolt moment of enlightenment. My brain and my life would be forever rerouted.

I WENT FROM IMPOVERISHED IN THOUGHT TO RICH IN SPIRIT TO WEALTHY IN REALITY!

From that point on, I was one of the "very rich." *I thought it and it was so.* I manifested a fortune just by changing my mind and erasing lazy mental habits. I hope this book will do the same for you. Fitzgeralds's observations of the "very rich" showed me how I needed to think and behave if I wanted to be rich myself. Fitzgerald, as my new spirit guide and mentor, taught me how to speak with a voice "full of money!" like Daisy Buchanan. To speak my wealth into existence. I finally understood who I needed to be to collect my treasures in the storehouses that are both in heaven and here on earth.

So, please, please read and re-read all of F. Scott Fitzgerald's work carefully. Truly understand what he meant in his novels and short stories. And then you too will be able to think and grow "very rich!"

Part of training our brains for future prosperity is the repetition of those new ideas and thoughts until they become part of our muscle memory.

SO LET'S REVIEW THE FITZGERALDIAN PRINCIPLES OF THE VERY RICH:

1) **Yes! I do believe that we, the "very rich," do possess early and often**. Meaning we take what The Universe has to offer, and we enjoy the hell out of it without dreadful apologies or useless guilt. We simply do not give into the temptation of believing in the twin fantasies of poverty and misery.

2) **As Fitzgerald observed, the rich are also soft and cynical.** We are leather and lace. Velvet and steel. We're ruthlessly cuddlesome because we are so open to miracles and because we intuitively trust the messy process of creation. People and money are attracted to our primal

energy. Why do you think the wealthy have such supermundane sex lives?

3) **We not only attract money but love and affection.** Raising your vibe has many benefits; a splendid and varied love life is just one. Because trust and optimism are as sexy as any musk. Our open and abundant natures truly magnetize everything to us. The Universe always returns our affection and attraction by fulfilling every one of our dreams, no matter how big or small. **STOP! Read this section seven times before proceeding in the book.**

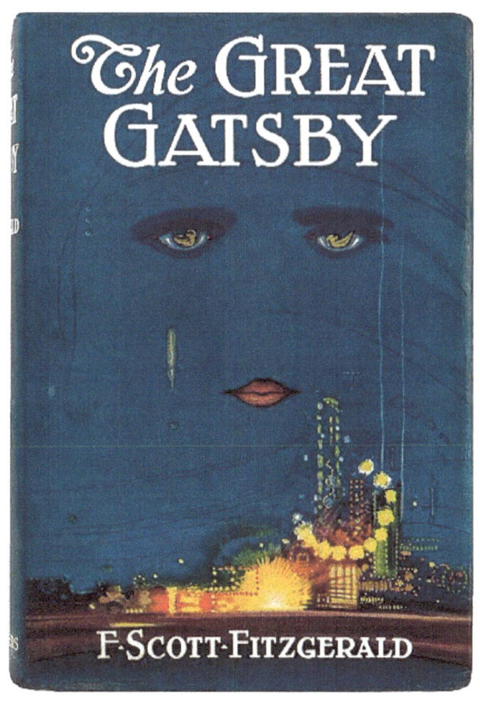

Image courtesy of Wikimedia Commons.

THERE IS NO SECRET TO MANIFESTATION!

The truly wealthy in mindset can think, “Gee, I would like a new private jet.” And voila! The very next day, they are flying over the North Pole in a brand new Airbus 380, eating caviar and cream cheese on water crackers while throating Cristal. The “very rich” simply think something and they snap their fingers or stomp their foot and like magic, it happens! But it is better than magic. It is money! And money can make anything happen. It is the force that makes the world go ‘round. (That’s not just a song.)

These miracles happen so effortlessly for us because, as F. Scott mentioned, the "very rich” take possession early and often. We “name it and claim it” which is the *FIFTH & FINAL LAW OF ABUNDANCE*. But I will explain all that in a later chapter. For now digest the fact that **the rich do not bitch**. We really don’t. We are too busy enjoying our 500-foot yachts in the Mediterranean, eating tender strips of Wagyu beef hand-fed to us by Gordon Ramsey. Way too busy making YouTube videos of ourselves, shouting and screaming as we bungee into orange canyons over emerald rivers.

While you might begrudge us our exploits, we do not give two flips about what the poor-minded think of us. We cannot waste our mental energy on such trivial matters or illusions. That is why the "very rich," like Fitzgerald said, think we are better than you.

BECAUSE WHAT WE THINK, WE CREATE.

This is the very essence of manifestation. To spend all our time feeling guilty for having mastered THE LAWS OF ABUNDANCE is a waste of time and energy. The only real sins in the eyes of The Universe. Also, why feel guilty? Why worry what others are thinking about us? They too could have store houses of treasure if they would just break their addictions to negative thinking. Poverty is an illusion, albeit a convincing one.

Sorry if this rubs you the wrong way. It is true. The "very rich" are better at manifesting wealth than the so called "poors." And do you not admit that being rich is better than being poor or even middle class? Those are just the facts of life. Why hate us for refusing your false reality? In fact, this hate of the rich is quite possibly why you are still poor or at least not as rich as you would like to be.

But more on that later.

Unlike those of you still ignorant to *THE LAWS OF ABUNDANCE,* the rich know our values and we know that people who understand *The Laws* are more evolved spiritual beings than those who don't respect them.

Again, I know for many of you this might be hard to hear but that's just how quantum physics work

On a personal note, it's okay to know that you are better at manifesting abundance than others. It's okay to feel good about yourself and all the things you have earned in your life by being spiritual. Letting someone make you feel guilty about this is a trap made for fools set by wretches.

Repeat to yourself upon waking every morning or when you feel the urge to complain: "The rich don't bitch." And the truly rich, the true masters of manifestation, especially don't bitch about their haters. We know they exist, but we do not give an ounce of our energy to such toxicity. We just blissfully accept the fact that success breeds envy. Other people's envy is a surefire sign *The Laws* are working.

IT'S LIKE THE OLD PARABLE GOES:

The wolf does not care what the sheep think. Instead, the wolf devours the meaty pleasures that are placed at her feet by an infinitely generous Universe. And the wolf does not apologize for feasting upon her prey because she knows The Universe has unlimited resources, and she is simply sipping from an endless cup of divine energy that can be available to any and everyone if they would just wipe the sleep from their eyes and stop being so dang negative all the damn time.TO BECOME Truly Rich, First You Must not Hate The Richest among You. INsteaD You must FALL IN

Love WITH Them. because what You love, You will EVENTUALLY become.

I am so sick of seeing idealistic young people protesting Wall Street with their hysterical signs that say "Eat The Rich!" or "Stop Billionaires from Destroying our Planet!" These children are fools! Do these kids not realize that your brain will not allow you to become what you hate? They are literally programming their own minds to never be rich when they grow up! They might as well be frying their brains on drugs.

NEGATIVITY IS WORSE THAN SHOOTING HEROIN!

Do these poor souls realize they will never manifest wealth carrying on like that? Do you think The Universe wants to reward such hate? Do you think The Universe wants to do anything else but slap these ingrates across the face with a life of poverty and despair?

What gall! What insolence! No one likes sore losers, not even an all-loving Universe. The first step on your path to dreamlike prosperity is to make peace with your jealousy of the rich. Stop hating. Stop blaming us for all your problems. Stop complaining that you do not have healthcare and that you pay more taxes than we do. Ever heard the expression: "Hate the game, not the player?" (Let me go one step further and say hate your own negative thoughts that keep you poor. There is nothing to hate even about this game. Play it joyfully and with positivity and love.)

WE ARE NOT YOUR ENEMY. WE ARE YOUR INSPIRATION!

We are what you could become if you can get over your impoverished thinking. Because what you think and say you become. Live *THE LAWS OF ABUNDANCE!* Read them. Repeat them. Say them so much that they encode your very DNA and you pass them down to all your descendants.

So you might be asking, "Aurora, how do I, when I am scalding my hands at my job at Starbucks everyday making lattes for these rich SOBs, make peace with the fact that I am barely scraping by in this economy while billionaires are on their yachts splashing Champagne and spilling caviar? How do I remain positive about that?"

First of all, not all billionaires love yachts. What a nasty stereotype. Most of us prefer private jets. Stop thinking we are all like Jeffery Epstein or Elizabeth Holmes. Stop listening to podcasts and watching Netflix specials about these trashy sociopaths. Stop treating us as if we are not good people!

STUDY THE RICH & STORIED LIVES OF JP MORGAN & JD ROCKEFELLER

Image courtesy of Wikimedia Commons

The great JP Morgan striking a photographer with his cane.

Study-up on these true gentlemen of the Gilded Age. Learn to open your heart to billionaires. Fall in love with their ambition. Admire their vision. Believe you can be them. But first, you have to kill your envy of the "very rich."

STOP BLAMING US FOR YOUR SMALL DREAMS AND POOR LIFE CHOICES.

Image courtesy of Wikimedia Commons

Time Saving Truth from Falsehood and Envy by François Lemoyne (1737) Completed on the day before the artist's suicide.

Please check yourself and your envy. Kill the green-eyed monster inside you. That's how you start on the true journey to wealth and happiness. You must show your lesser self who is boss. You must fill your heart with love and admiration towards the people intrepid enough to make their own dreams come true.

You must admit that you are just not there yet, and that you also are a big enough person to cheer on those of us who have mastered *THE LAWS OF ABUNDANCE*.

Murder your envy and all the falsehood that tells you to hate the "very rich" —that is, if you want to become "very rich" yourself.

INCOMING!

I HAVE A SUDDEN MESSAGE CHANNELED DIRECTLY FROM INFINITE INTELLIGENCE!

"America, you must exorcise your hatred and disdain for the billionaire with these exercises:

1) **Gorge** on the lifestyles of the rich and famous. Follow them on Twitter. Read their Wikipedia pages. You cannot be too obsessed with their lives. This will program your brain to be open enough to handle their level of abundance—to expand your threshold for good fortune.

2) **Splurge** and buy a Gucci handbag if you identify as a woman. Buy the most expensive, most recent iPhone if you identify as a man. This will show The Universe that you are ready for the abundant softness that only the rich can truly appreciate.

3) **Pour** over every image in *The Robb Report* and *Vanity Fair*. Cut out the images that kindle your desire and keep them in a file folder. We will put them to work for you in a later chapter. It is important that you buy at least of these magazines and capture these images.

4) **Study** the *Forbes Wealthiest People in the World Lists*. Scratch out the name of the wealthiest person and write in your name. Cut out your photo and place it over said billionaire's face—not with malice but with admiration. Frame this image and keep it on your "prosperity altar." (Which we will build together in the final chapter.)

5) **Read** and re-read Warren Buffet's biography. Follow his routines minus eating McDonald's three times a week.

6) **Buy** *The Art of War* on audiobooks and listen to it while you are on the treadmill. Know that all business is art and war. Paint and fight accordingly.

7) **Start** a Pinterest board of dream houses and exotic vacations that you cannot imagine affording with your current station in life. Go big! The more impossible, the better. Find images that make you ache with wanting.

8) **Allow** the images to kindle into a deep, almost painful longing. Burn with this desire deep within your loins. Marshall these painful cravings when you say your mantra every day as the sunsets: "I am rich! I am rich! I am rich!" Then say it in French, "Je suis riche! Je suis riche! Je suis riche!"

9) **Write** this incantation down as you say it. Before the sun dips out of sight, fold the paper into threes, and burn it over a white candle as night falls.

10) **Take** the ashes and spread them into fresh, living water. As you sprinkle them, you say again, "I am rich. I am rich. I am rich. Three by three, so mote it be. "

11) Then you **fill your heart with genuine love** towards the rich because "very soon" you will become one of them. You love them as you love yourself. If you can just keep your full of this love, your head full of your dreams, and your mind free of impoverished thoughts, The Universe will start to take notice.

Now doing this ritual every night might seem a little over the top. But you have a lifetime of negative programming you have to overwrite. Doing this nightly will help you erase and repair millions of negative vibes that you have already programed into the matrix over your lifetime.

TRUST ME, ONCE YOU SEE YOUR DREAMS COMING TRUE THIS WON'T SEEM SO STUPID.

Soon you will have to brace yourself for the seismic shifts in your life as the infinite flow of money will rush to your bank account, like iron filings to a magnet, sperm to an egg, chickens on a June bug!"

EVERYTHING COMES FROM NOTHING.

EVEN YOU!

Image courtesy of Wikimedia

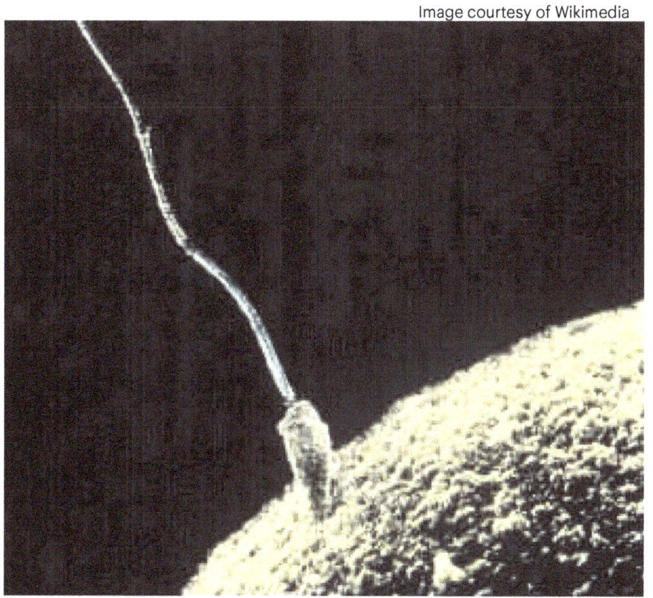

The two key components to manifesting anything out of oblivion, from babies to birthday wishes, is explosive desire and relentless determination.

FOURTH LAW OF ABUNDANCE:
SEE IT TO BE IT.

Image courtesy of Wikimedia Commons

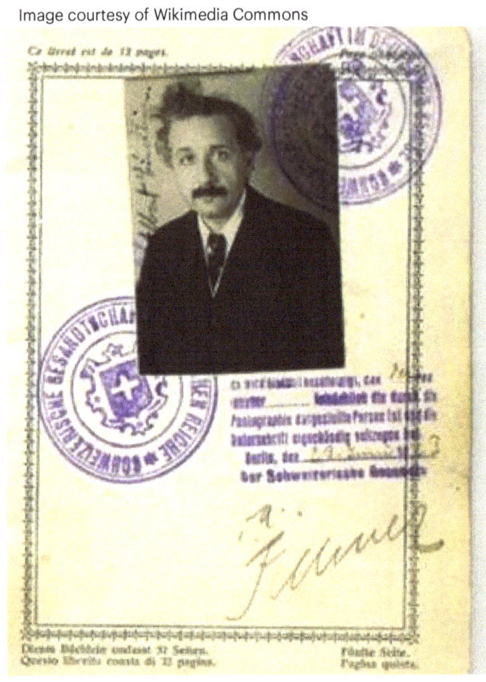

AS a psychic medium and professional channeler, I have had, on more than one occasion, the pleasure of speaking with Albert Einstein. (Yes, that Albert Einstein!) And he is so funny. I mean, would you imagine the genius who totally reconfigured our concept of space, time, and gravity, would be such a card? A total stitch. At least he was before we got sideways about String Theory. If you want to know the truth, the man can such a know-it-all. And an ass. But more about that later.

When Albert first came through, we totally hit it off. Like minds think alike and such. He initially came through from the other side on a quest to bestow upon me complete understanding of his Law of Relativity ($e=mc^2$).

Just look at how elegant that equation is and how powerful that one thought from this great man was. Can you even imagine the impact those four characters have had on the earth plane?

Elegant thoughts, like Einstein's Theory of Relativity, can change everything.

But Albert will be the first to tell you that it took lots of mental discipline to distill his ideas into such elegant thoughts.

The same will hold doubly, maybe triply, true for you.

Albert has told me many times in our afterlife sessions: "True genius comes from being able to take what you see in your mind and make it a reality." Albert spent his entire lifetime trying to take what he saw in his brilliant mind and distill it down. He then tried to use this one simple formula to explain the wonder of The Universe to a world full of naysayers and dullards. Men of war who used it to build a bomb. I told Albert, "Newsflash: Maybe if you wanted everyone to understand your idea, it shouldn't have been an equation. People are terrible at math!"

This got a good laugh out of both of us.

God, we used to be so close. That was until my ability to manifest true wealth and abundance eventually tore us apart. Like it sadly does to most friends when one isn't ready to raise their vibration. Ironically, Albert's early messages to me from the Spirit Realm almost predicted that this would happen. But when it did, I was still just as surprised and upset that he turned on me.

I guess everyone comes into our lives for a reason and Albert came into mine to teach me the "power of elegant thinking."

TALKING TO ALBERT ACROSS THE ETHERS TAUGHT ME THAT ELEGANT THOUGHTS ARE THE KEY TO MANIFESTING A BETTER REALITY FOR OURSELVES AND OUR UNDERLINGS.

We should all take our queues from Albert on this one (even though he did eventually turn his back on me like he did to most of the women in his life) if we are to learn how to think more positively. We must think more elegantly. Clear your brain of all detritus and flotsam. Think only clean, smooth thoughts. Keep yourself vibrating as fine as a bee's wing and your dreams will take off. Your thoughts will pollinate the world and bloom into explosions of color. Sadly, while elegant thinking is truly the lesson here, you must ignore Albert when it comes to quantum physics. Oh, how he liked to bend my ear about the dangers of exploiting quantum mechanics — the "spooky science" he liked to call it.

YOU CAN HOLD POSITIVE THOUGHTS EVEN WHEN YOU ARE MAD AT SOMEONE.

At my lake house in the middle of winter, while my dear friends, Nancy and Donny Regan, are out on the lake. Left behind, arguing with Albert Einstein about *THE LAWS OF ABUNDANCE*. Such a pain in my neck that guy. But also what a sweetheart when he wanted to be. I miss our talks. They not only strengthened my knowledge of The Universe, but they taught me the importance of removing negative people from my life. Once again proving that there are no mistakes in this Cosmos. Only lessons.

“Unthinking respect for authority is the greatest enemy of truth.”

Albert Einstein

Image courtesy of Wikimedia Commons

ALBERT ONCE TOLD ME, "AURORA, ENOUGH WITH THE QUANTUM BULLSHIT! YOU SOUND LIKE AN ASSHOLE WHEN YOU SAY SUCH THINGS."

"Please, Albert," I said. "Stay in your lane and watch how you talk to me. I do not deal with abusive spirits!"

"I am in my lane! I refuse to accept quantum mechanics because I like to think the moon is there even if I am not looking at it!"

"But even in your death, sweet Albert, you still think this way?" I would try to cajole him. "Even as you dance upon the fields of pure potentiality and set sail on the oceans of oblivion, you still don't believe in quantum mechanics?"

"The moon is real!" he gruffed. "So are atoms!"

What Einstein was referring to are the quantum theories developed *after* his beloved $e=mc^2$. In short, most quantum theories say that atoms are not real. That they somehow (we don't quite know how) form a Universe of potentialities rather than one set law of definitive reality. They blink in and out of existence. They are wave and particle. Depends now aha you want them to be. Our desires determine the outcome.

Einstein hated this notion with a white-hot passion when he was alive, and it seems much hasn't changed, even in death.

"Quantum theory yields much," Albert chastised me during one of our afterlife sessions. "But it hardly brings us close to the Old One's secrets. I, in any case, am convinced He does not play dice with The Universe."

"Oh, Albert."

A great visionary like Albert can still become entangled in his own negative thoughts and refuse the truth.

Even Einstein doesn't know everything.

So do not sit here, reading my book thinking you have the "Mysteries of The Multi-verses" all figured out. Because you do not. In fact, you might want to get a pencil and pad and start taking notes. This is where you, like Einstein, are going to be challenged by my fantastic downloads from the Quantum Realm.

NOT TO BE A NOODGE, BUT GO NOW! GET A NOTEBOOK AND A PENCIL. I CAN WAIT.

If you are to understand my complex theories, you must internalized them. And that requires note-taking (Not just highlighting in the book. That does nothing but ruin the book!).

So now that you are back with pencil and notebook handy, make sure you date the page and get to taking notes about these ideas to study later. Here, copy this verbatim:

If I am ever going to defeat my own negative thinking and finally start thinking positively and manifesting the billions of dollars that The Universe has in store for me, I am going to have to read and re-read THE LAWS OF ABUNDANCE at least a hundred times.

Now that we are clear on what must be done to master THE LAWS, let me describe to you the ideas given to me by The Universe. But you, like Einstein, may not want to understand it. You may say this is all just a bunch of New Age who-ha. You may say, "Aurora, what about critical thinking?"

And I would clap back: "No one likes a critic!"

Actually it is not necessary that you have an advanced degree in astrophysics to master *THE LAWS OF ABUNDANCE*. Just know that we are all vibrations, even the atoms of our atoms, and because of this, we can literally manifest things out of thin air if we are vibrating at a high enough level. Doubt like the doubt cast by Einstein's ghost, lowers our vibration. So mind who you keep company with and who you listen to—even if you don't believe a word they say, just being around their negative thoughts and words can decrease your vibrational level; and thus ruin your ability to manifest your dreams.

You just have to believe in what you are doing. (Always be positive. Resist everyone's doubts. Which I know is a constant fight. Even I struggle with it sometimes.) So let me gently guide you into understanding what even Einstein couldn't comprehend, let me try to channel the clearest I have ever channeled infinite wisdom for you. What follows comes directly from Source:

QUANTUM PARTICLES ARE TINIER THAN EVEN ELECTRONS. YOU CAN'T EVEN IMAGINE HOW TINY.

To delve into this quantum realm we are talking about a system with the typical mass (m), speed (v), and distance (d) is on the order of Plank's constant (h) [$6.626X10^{-34}$ joule-seconds]. Don't even try to visualize this. Your monkey mind will only fight you.

Unfortunately, most people's brains are stuck in classical Newtonian reality. (Exactly where Einstein would obviously prefer for us all to remain. Perhaps because the quantum realm might overturn someone's elegant little equation.) Regardless, if you remain a "normal" human with "normal" negative thoughts, you will never raise your vibration. And the mass(m) of your neural transmitter molecules and their speed(v) and distance(d) across your synapses are about two orders too big in magnitude to effect even the largest quantum particle or wave.

However, there is hope! If you, like me and my wealthy cohort, raise your vibrations (avoid all negative thoughts, people, foods, and places) to the highest levels, to the levels of most billionaires, you can transcend the Newtonian prison of your brain, and if you think positively enough, visualize hard enough, your own quantum strings will vibrate in symphony with the strings of the highest realms.

Angels will sing with you.

You will be able to manifest your thoughts into vibrations that affect the strings of your own reality. I don't care what Einstein says. This is real. And it works. The quantum field is a thing. Just ask Jack Dorsey or Elon Musk. We live in a hologram — a simulation that your mind programs with its thoughts. Have you not seen *The Matrix?*

So rid yourself of negative thought. Practice positivity and visualize what you truly want; and your dreams will bear fruit. A real toad will appear in your imaginary garden.

ALL YOU HAVE TO DO IS SEE IT TO BE IT.

"This is not physics!" Einstein haunted me for months once I had proclaimed my mastery over the quantum realm. "It is magical thinking! " he bemoaned. "Primitive folk magic!" he complained. "Ignorant superstition!" he shouted.

Einstein would literally stand over my bed in the middle of the night, his hair, crazy, all over the place, dripping in the chains of his own negative thoughts, looking like Jacob Marley's ghost.

"It is solipsism pure and simple!" Einstein would hector me. (The man wrecked our otherworldly friendship with his pessimism and "science.")

So I did what I do with all the negative people in my life:

I banished the ghost of Albert Einstein.

FOREVER.

Important lesson here: There are going to be tons of know-it-all "keyboard scientists" who are going to "fact check" you when it comes to activating THE LAWS OF ABUNDANCE in your life. They are just trying to lower your vibration.

Don't let them.

Do not give one single thought or breath to negative people.

Don't join them in their tangled thoughts.

Even if they are someone who thinks they are as smart as Albert Einstein himself.

Because when you don't believe in your own power to change the world, you actually have none. Do not let the haters psyche you out. Do not let anyone tell you there is a "Secret" to anything.

There isn't.

THERE IS ONLY YOU.

My lake house garden during the bleakest of winters. Everything blooms perpetually when you stay positive and work *THE LAWS OF ABUNDANCE*. Do flowers bloom around you or do they die? That's the real question here.

THE UNIVERSE SPEAKS IN METAPHORS AND IMAGES. IF YOU WANT YOUR DREAMS ANSWERED, YOU HAVE TO SPEAK TO THE UNIVERSE IN ITS LANGUAGE.

Remember when I told you to scour *The Robb Report* and *Vanity Fair, to* clip out images that represent your heart's desire? I think I told you to keep them in a file folder. Remember that?

Good.

Because I need you to put this book down (Use a bookmark. Do not dog-ear a sacred text or break the spine!) and go find that file folder full of your clippings, while you are doing that also grab a poster board, craft scissors, magic markers, glue sticks, and if you really want to have fun, some paint or glitter.

We are going to make a vision board.

But first, you must read and understand the final and most important *LAW OF ABUNDANCE. THE FIFTH LAW.* And from there, you will rewrite the story of your life.

Image courtesy of Wikimedia Commons

“If you meet the Buddha
on the road,
kill him.”

Linji Yixuan

FIFTH LAW OF ABUNDANCE:

NAME IT. AND CLAIM IT.

We are co-creators with The Universe. What we think about, we bring about. We merely have to name our dreams to claim them. This is the *FIFTH AND PENULTIMATE LAW*. Some say it is the only *LAW*, which is why it is so important to use only positive words and positive thoughts in all your waking hours. You must banish the demons of doubt and the banshees of pessimism once and for all. Your tantrums and constant complaining are a form of spiritual thumb sucking. Being negative might soothe your hurt feelings in the moment, but it makes you look babyish to The Universe and moves the very teeth of destiny out of alignment!

You must be positive if you ever want your life to be okay.

By understanding that our minds actually affect quantum reality, we can raise our frequency and manifest our dreams out of the chaos. We can dream ourselves into becoming the next Ivanka Trump or Hetty Green or J. Paul Getty Sr. (The man who was too wily to be duped by his grandson's kidnappers). If we think positively enough, if we allow our optimism to guide, the world will open to us like a shucked oyster, full of delicious flesh and gorgeous peals. That is the beauty of *THE LAWS OF ABUNDANCE*. They work for everyone. But sadly, not everyone works for them. It is far too popular these days with Facebook and Twitter to be negative, to be mean, to be skeptical, and to get attention by playing the victim of circumstance, which is just an illusion because we create our own reality. We draw into our lives what we are aligned to spiritually and energetically.

WE REAP WHAT WE SOW.

Now that you understand that The Universe responds directly to you naming your dreams and goals by allowing you to claim them, you are ready to make your vision board.

For years creative visualization has been a big part of the New Age and Positive Psychology community. Problem is most people have been doing it all wrong, which is why their lives don't change after one "crafternoon" of magazine cut-outs and poster boards.

First, have you ever seen most people's attempts at credible vision boards? Well, I have. People are always wanting to show them to me when I am keynoting at psychic fairs and New Age conferences, and I am sorry to report that most vision boards are pure trash. No wonder so many of you struggle with manifestation. No wonder so many of you report to me that your lives are "absolute shit shows!" Your vision boards look like drunk kindergartners made them.

Do you think The Universe wants to reward sloppy, uninspired work? Then why do you think your half-assed artistic efforts will manifest your dreams?

NO ONE LIKES SLAP-DASH, HAPHAZARD EFFORTS.

Applying carelessly cut-out images or photos from poor people magazines like *US Weekly, The National Enquirer, USA Today,* and *People* are big no-nos; using recycled cardboard instead of splurging on crisp, white poster board or using old markers (brown markers are a big no!) or being cheap and relying on crappy left-over paints from random craft projects instead of carefully choosing a Pantone palette, will doom your vision board to be ignored by The Universe. Because who is inspired by tackiness? Definitely not Infinite Intelligence, I can tell you that.

This begs the question of whether or not to use glitter. (I can't even believe that we are having this conversation.)

YES, YOU MUST USE GLITTER.

How else do you think the board will reflect your vibrations back out into The Universe? Your vision board must have all the tiny reflections of light provided by tastefully applied glitter to work. With that said, a little glitter goes a long way. And I think that's where the confusion is when it comes to crafting vision boards. Just know that glitter is the essential ingredient if you expect your vision board to transmit your desires via photons to The Universe.

GLITTER IS THE "SECRET CHIK-FIL-A SAUCE," AS THE KIDS LIKE TO SAY.

The best glitter to use is" Elizabeth Craft Designs Silk Microfine Glitter, 14-Gram, Cool Diamond." This stuff rocks. It's as close to pixie dust as you are ever going to get while you on the earth plane. It not only gives your board a gorgeous shimmer, but it also super-charges your intentions and speeds up manifestation by broadcasting your dreams and desired into photons. Be careful with application; too much can also have the opposite, very distorting effect.

Once I put too much glitter on a vision board trying to manifest a second husband. And I not only manifested a second husband, but then a lover, and then a second lover, and then a third husband. I finally had to rip up the vision board after marrying my third husband because my high school boyfriend showed up on our doorstep with an engagement ring in his open palm and a tear in his eye. Too much glitter can over-broadcast and distort your intentions. Trust me on this one. Secondly and just as importantly, I recommend that you mine your images from just two magazines: *Vanity Fair* and *The Robb Report*. Cutting out your images from just these two magazines will increase your success rate by almost 90%. After over 30 years of manifesting millions of dollars for myself and my heirs, I find these two publications reliably create the best financial outcomes.

Sure, you can use *O Magazine, Magnolia, or Martha Stewart,* or even *Dwell and Wallpaper,* but for whatever reason, lifestyle or interior design magazines don't work as well as magazines that profile the actual lives of the rich and famous.

IT'S A VIBRATION THING FOR SURE

A "basic" vision board that lacks glitter and imagination. It's just a bunch of lazy cut-outs from lame magazines. Do you think The Universe likes this decoupage of boring ideas? Where's the craftsmanship? The pizzazz? The energy?

FINALLY, LET'S TALK GLUE. (A METAPHOR FOR DARK ENERGY IF THERE EVER WAS)

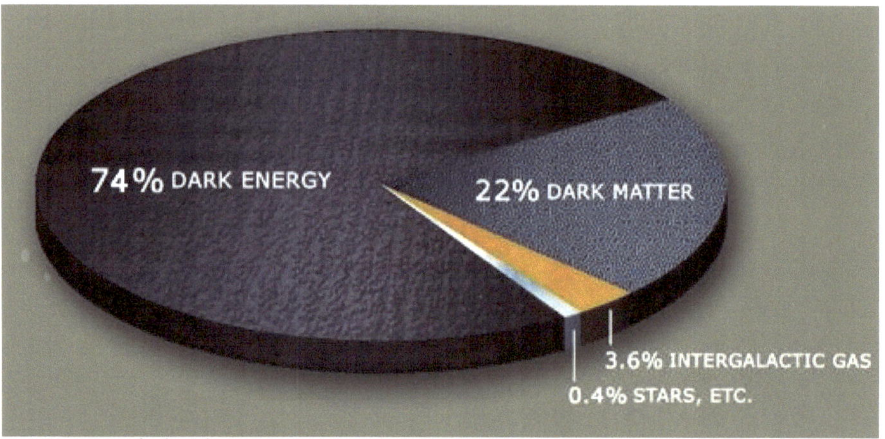

Image courtesy of Wikimedia Commons

Glue is what makes your whole vision board work. It literally holds it all together. Like the dark energy that holds our reality together. The Universe is very sensitive to how respectful you are with this particular metaphor. It's very important not to make a mess. Messy glue is why many vision boards end up so impotent.

While The Universe is also a form of self-knowing Chaos, as a system, The Universe hates sticky, over-glued vision boards. For years people swore by their hot glue guns as the ultimate vision board staple. But I find them to be tiresome. (Both the guns and the gun owners.) They are, more times than not, just a hot mess. Instead, keep your boards simple; stick with the classic "Elmer's Disappearing Purple School Glue Sticks, Washable, 0.21 Ounce for Kids."

It's easy to use, works well, and if you make a mess, it's washable.

Now that you have your materials handy, it is important to use a fresh pair of craft scissors. I often buy a new pair for big projects when I really have to pull things out of thin air. And then get to crafting a beautifully designed, well-executed vision board. Once you have the imagery where you want it, once it is just trembling with inspiration, lightly blot the glue stick all over your completed board, and then tease the images with glitter. (Not too much, but just enough.) Notice how the sparkles catch the light. Now imagine in your mind's eye how these visualizations will feel once they materialize in your life.

FEELS GOOD, RIGHT?

Now this is so important: Say aloud the names of all the things you want in your life. Then claim a date that it will all materialize. Jot it down right on the board as you say it. Make sure you use a nice marker and good penmanship. We still need this to look nice. (This is the part most people forget to do and it matters! Your board will not work without it.)

Next, shake off the excess glitter and keep your vision board, maybe even frame it, on your prosperity altar.

What? You don't have a prosperity altar? Uh, how do you expect your vision board to recharge and send out vibrations that The Universe will use to re-arrange itself to bring you exactly what you are asking for (no matter how small or big) if you don't have a prosperity altar?

If you don't have an altar, here's how to build one:

HOW TO MAKE YOUR PROSPERITY ALTAR

1. **Choose the space.** I like your bedroom. The top of your dresser or vanity works fine. It needs to be in a visible location. Please do not hide it in your closet. There should be no shame in your game when it comes to asking The Universe to unleash its flow of abundance on you.
2. **Clean the space.** Light a smudge stick and waft away the muddy energy. Then make it pretty. Fresh flowers and candles and your favorite chocolates will do.
3. **Place your vision board** at the center of the altar.
4. **Taste a piece of your "altar chocolate"** every time you look at the board. Make it a multi-sensory experience. Smell the flowers. Feel the joy of making your dreams real. Let your desires melt with the chocolate in your mouth.
5. **Chat with The Universe.** (Don't complain! Prayers of gratitude only!) Tell the Cosmos what you want. Listen. See if The Universe answers you back.
6. **Because It will**. Oh, It will!

REPEAT EVERY 5 MINUTES:

MY INNER-VERSE IS ALSO YOUR OUTER-VERSE.

Image courtesy of iStockPhoto

What is happening in your heart and mind co-creates reality. "As above, so below," as the witches used to say. It's all the same principles. Master this occult thought and you are on your way to working *THE LAWS OF ABUNDANCE* and untold billions!

ABOUT THE AUTHOR

AURORA ABERDEEN is a pioneer in science fiction romance literature and philosophy. She is the author of over twenty-five novels and twenty-two self-help books translated in over thirty languages, published in over fifty countries. Ms. Aberdeen is the recipient of the prestigious" Pleiadian Star of Wonder" for her work as a U.S. Remote Viewer. She resides in Victoria, British Columbia, where she lives with her two Shih Tzus, Hercules and Hera. Ms. Aberdeen enjoys keeping flowers in full bloom and communicating with the local pods of orca, particularly "J-pod."

www.ingramcontent.com/pod-product-compliance
Lightning Source LLC
LaVergne TN
LVHW052304100826
845147LV00006B/675

* 9 7 8 0 9 7 2 6 5 8 8 6 7 *